INTO THE
LIGHT

The Chaplain Gerry Story

MONICA BURNEY

ILLUMIFY
MEDIA.COM

Into the Light
Copyright © 2022 by Monica Burney

Published by
Illumify Media Global
www.IllumifyMedia.com
"Let's bring your book to life!"

Library of Congress Control Number: 2022913008

Paperback ISBN: 978-1-955043-83-0

Cover design by Debbie Lewis
Printed in the United States of America

To our dear children, Mike, Vanessa, and Hillary, daughter-in law, Katie, and our precious grandchildren, Ryan, Nate, and Gracie:

We thank God for our beautiful family. You are each a special treasure to us, and so deeply loved.

May the God of hope fill you with all joy and peace as you trust in him, so that you may overflow with hope by the power of the Holy Spirit.

~Romans 15:13 NIV

CONTENTS

ACKNOWLEDGMENTS

With appreciation to Geoff Stone, Aaron Watson, and Debbee Freeman for their time investment and insightful input to help the book along its journey to what it needed to become.

INTRODUCTION

Over the past several years or so, several people have suggested that I write a book about my life. They had heard me share stories from my life experiences that were especially memorable to me. I felt very uncomfortable about the idea because for one thing, I didn't see my life as fascinating enough to fill up the pages of an entire book. For another thing, even though countless others have written their autobiography, for me anyway, being somewhat of a private person, to write one about myself felt a bit self-aggrandizing.

I came to realize, however, that even though it would recount stories from my life, it would also provide an opportunity to shine the spotlight where it truly belonged: on God's redeeming love, His message of hope, and the light of His truth.

Although I came to a point of feeling at peace about my story being told, I still didn't feel compelled to write it. I asked my wife, Monica, if she would take on the task. After prayerful consideration, she willingly accepted the challenge and set out to tell the story using her words, yet with my voice.

It is the hope and prayer of both Monica and I that this book will inspire, encourage, and bless everyone that takes the time to read through its pages. Most of all, we hope God will be pleased, honored, and glorified.

Gerry Burney

But you are a chosen race, a royal priesthood, a holy nation, a people for God's own possession, so that you may proclaim the excellencies of Him who has called you out of darkness into His marvelous light.

~1 Peter 2:9 NASB

THE EARLY YEARS

Although a good portion of my growing up years was spent in Northern California, some of my most formative years were spent on a farm in the Central Valley. After spending my first two years of life in Napa, California, our family moved to Santa Rosa, after my brother, Steve, came along. We lived there until the end of my fifth grade year. We then moved to the small, rural, agricultural community of Chowchilla, where I attended Dairyland Elementary School—a school that sadly became notorious many years later.

In 1976 the school experienced a horrific crime. The school bus driver and twenty-six children, ages five to fourteen, were kidnapped. They were transferred to a box truck that was subsequently buried in a quarry in Livermore, California. The kidnappers hoped to get a ransom for their return. After about 16 hours underground, the driver and children dug themselves out and escaped.

Chowchilla is also where I learned much about hard work and seeing the fruit of one's labors. Starting in sixth grade, I was doing typical chores on our forty-acre farm, as well as helping out on my Uncle Dick and Aunt Velda's farm. Additionally, I spent time doing chores at my Grandpa Steve and Grandma Grace's ranch. My Grandpa Steve farmed cotton and alfalfa. By eighth and ninth grade, I was harvesting corn, baling hay, helping to raise white face and black angus cattle, and hunting rabbits with a 4-10 shotgun. I was paid fifty cents per a rabbit, but the primary reason for shooting them was because they were chewing on our trees. I also handpicked cotton with the Bracero workers, earning three-and-a-half cents per pound. The Braceros were paid two-and-a-half cents a pound, but they got first pickings—I had to glean what was left.

Gerry and brother, Steve, saying, "Cheese!"

Gerry went through a phase in early grade school when he wore his favorite shirt to school every day for a few weeks. He would smuggle it out the front door in the morning and change shirts on the way to school. His mom was surprised to get a call from his concerned teacher one day asking if everything was okay at home and if he owned any other shirts!

My Uncle Dick not only was a good farmer, but also a very good mechanic. He made most of his money picking cotton for other people. Although mechanical pickers had been invented already, most small farms did not have access to one. He was one of the first to own a cotton-picking machine. He was also an innovator. He liked to experiment with grafting apple, plum, and pear trees together.

Early grade school portrait Dairyland Elementary School, Chowchilla

I enjoyed life on the farm, but I knew there had to be more to life than just school and chores. So I tried out for the Little League baseball team, the Cotton Oilers. I was the worst player on the team, but that did not prevent me from making my mark. Even though I couldn't hit, catch, or throw a ball, I did end up having the best on-base percentage of the entire team. How was this possible, you ask?

School Days 55-56

Gerry, age ten

Gerry with his mom, dad, Grandpa Steve, and brother, Steve, on the farm.

The Burney boys in Burney

There is a bit of a family history with Burney, California. Gerry's parents and brother lived there after the parents retired. Daughter Vanessa visited another set of grandparents in nearby Cassel every July while growing up. It is there that she learned to fly fish and later became a fly fishing guide for a time at Fall River.

Back then you needed fifteen players to field a team. As it turned out, it wasn't easy to find fifteen players, so although I was the last person selected, I made the team. As the season progressed, I never got to play—I just warmed the bench. Then, one day, besides me only eight players showed up, so the coach put me in right field and I was the last to bat.

Again, I couldn't catch, throw, or hit to save my life. When I got up to bat, I was kind of slow to catch on at first. In Little League, however, pitchers aren't very refined and can sometimes throw some pretty wild pitches. So I got hit numerous times at bat by wild pitches, which meant I got on base pretty often. That's when I realized the one thing I could do fairly well was run, and steal bases. By the end of the season, I had the best on-base percentage of anyone on the team. Go figure.

In my first year at Chowchilla High School, I rode the bus from the farm—about ten miles away. When we arrived at school that first week, a campus security man got on the bus and announced that as we departed, each of us would be searched for weapons— both knives and guns. Suddenly, there was the loud clanking sound as many guns and knives hit the floor of the bus. Gangs were all over campus, but in those days, no one ever violently attacked anyone. It was a pride thing more than a protection thing to belong to a gang. I was always the youngest, smallest kid in class, at both high schools I attended—you might even say a runt—so I was an easy target for upperclassmen's shenanigans.

While in ninth grade, I attended a youth group at the church where my uncle and aunt belonged, but I really was only there to meet girls. Although I was interested in girls, I was shy and found it hard to date. When I was in tenth grade, we moved back to Santa Rosa. My parents intermittently attended church, but my dad told us flat out that he was there only to network with others in the community for his real estate business. Of course, we also attended for the occasional wedding or funeral. At home, even though we had a huge family Bible sitting on the coffee table, we never opened it, nor did we ever pray together.

I went to a church camp one summer—to meet girls. I would do whatever the other kids were doing, so I could fit in—even going into the lake to be baptized. However, I never really understood what it was all about.

I attended Montgomery High School and was second youngest in my class. My close friend, Vance Arnold, was on the cross-country and track teams. Although I wasn't athletic by any means, during my junior year he encouraged me to try running. I finished a two-mile run with the group and decided I would keep at it. It was 1962, and at age sixteen, I set the Northern California record for the 660-yard run at the Nor Cal High School Championships, beating the two favorites. I was told that the record still stands and the banner for the record still hangs in the high school gym. By the end of my senior year, I had won every 1320-yard race. For someone who started his athletic career as a runt and least likely to succeed in sports, it gave me great satisfaction to have found my stride in running. My fierce competitive spirit certainly helped.

I also was very disciplined thanks to my strong farm work ethic. Not only did my sense of discipline help me achieve my goals in running, it also helped me to save enough allowance to buy a car by age sixteen. In the summer going into my junior year, I went back to Chowchilla for a month, to work on my Grandpa Steve's place. While there, I tended the steers, shoveled manure, and pitchforked the hay for feed. I also hoed weeds in the walnut orchard, harvested corn, and stacked bales of hay.

When I returned home at the end of the summer, to my absolute horror, I discovered that my parents took my entire savings and bought me what they thought was a great car—a 1959 Nash Metropolitan! It was baby blue with a fake air scoop. Needless to say, I became the laughingstock at school. It took two more years of working at Chicken Delight before I could afford a cool car. While attending Santa Rosa Junior College, I paid $750.00 for a '56 Chevy. Today, it would be worth thousands.

The loathsome 1959 Nash Metropolitan

On the hood in "the hood": Gerry and Steve chillin' on Gerry's green and white '56 Chevy.

Over the years I have become somewhat of a car buff. At the risk of sounding like a braggadocio, I admit over the years I have owned a number of classic cars: a '56 Chevy, a T-bird, three different Porsche 914's (the poor man's Porsche), a Jaguar XJ6, and a Camaro. I was asked recently of all the vehicles I've owned what is my most favorite. I must say the Colorado. It is a 2006 red, four-door Chevy pick-up, nearing 250,000 miles. I can honestly say that I have been most satisfied with this vehicle, as it has the most miles of any vehicle I've ever owned, yet it's still humming along and has been such a practical, comfortable, workhorse of a vehicle.

13

THE AGE OF BECOMING

At college, I failed the English entry exam. I easily met the prerequisites for chemistry, physics, and trigonometry classes, but I was hopeless in English. I failed not only at the college level, but the high school level as well. In all truthfulness, the only class I was eligible for was English as a second language. I passed the foreign student English class the first time I took it. It took three more semesters, however, to finally pass the high school English requirement. Then came the tough one— college-level English. I passed it with a C and was very happy because when I graduated from junior college in 1965 only one semester of college-level English was required to graduate from a four-year college.

During my two years at Santa Rosa Junior College (SRJC), I worked forty-five to sixty hours per week as a cook for Boyd and Flo Miller at Chicken Delight at the rate of one dollar an hour. I took seventeen to eighteen units per semester and took summer classes as well. I ran cross-country and track for SRJC but was so burned out from working my full-time job and taking a full load at college that I had little time or energy to train for races.

At eighteen years old, I bought my first home in Montgomery Village for $13,000 and rented it out to a pro wrestler. In 1965, at nineteen years of age, I graduated from SRJC and went to summer school at San Jose State. I transferred to a local Chicken Delight and worked my way up to pizza maker, making a whopping $1.25 an hour. I bought a 1953 Mercury station wagon for only fifty dollars. It ran, but I bought it only to sleep in to save money, and, thankfully for me, the Chicken Delight in San Jose happened to have a place where I could shower.

Commute vehicle: Gerry's '49 Harley Davidson bike

To get around, I bought a 1949 Harley Davidson three-wheel motorcycle with wire wheels and a box in the back. I traveled from San Jose to Santa Rosa across the Golden Gate Bridge every other week for a quick visit. Top speed for the '49 Harley was 45 mph and back then helmets weren't required. In October 1965, I was again fairly burned out, so I joined the Air Force with my friend Keith Rohde. The war in Vietnam was fully engaged, and the military was glad to have us. I sold the house in Montgomery Village and put about $3,000 in my savings account. I went to boot camp in Lackland, Texas, and then was sent to Biloxi, Mississippi, for a year to study microwave radio.

Air Force recruit pic, age twenty

In 1966, I came back to Santa Rosa while on leave for two weeks. I married Carol, a girl I had dated in junior college and knew in high school. I picked up the '62 Ford Galaxy I had bought, and Carol and I drove to Mississippi. When I arrived in Biloxi, I found a place for fifty dollars a month, including furniture, electricity, gas, garbage, water and sewer. (That was really cheap even back then.) The room was over a garage, and I parked on the street. Being from California, we didn't mind at all living in a black neighborhood. However, I found out right away that the white sheriff didn't like it and our car kept getting ticketed. It was during this time that the non-violent civil rights demonstrations were taking place. In our all-black neighborhood, there was a white-owned grocery store with no black employees.

One day, I walked down to the grocery store to get a quart of milk. I arrived to find a long string of customers from the neighborhood all lined up outside of the store. I asked what was happening and was told it was a peaceful protest against the store owners because they wouldn't hire a black person—not even a box boy. The protest was designed so that everyone was to buy only one item. If they needed more items, they would get back in line. That way, they would tie up the cash register. Well, I was only there for milk, so I joined in with the others. As a result of the protest, the store owners ultimately changed their policy and hired two box boys from the neighborhood! It was a small step forward, but still a step in the right direction.

That was the first of three incidents in my life when I was spat upon. When the sheriff who had been ticketing my car because of my being color blind, caught wind that I had participated in the peaceful protest, he was upset and spat on me. This experience of being spat upon by him really opened my eyes to what black people were experiencing all the time in the South by many white people. It gave me an even greater empathy for their plight.

After finishing my year in Mississippi, I got orders to go to Las Vegas—not Nellis Air Force Base (AFB) close to Las Vegas but rather Angel's Peak radar station sixty miles outside of Vegas, up a nine-thousand-foot mountain. I was assigned to a room on Angel's Peak with Rich Pyles, who was from Los Angeles. After a few months, I rented an apartment close to the Strip on Chicago Avenue and moved Carol out to join me.

We had only one car, so I would jog to and from our apartment each day in full military dress and boots to save money. Carol got a job at Avis. I decided to further my education at the University of Nevada (UNLV). I ran for the UNLV cross-country team as a rabbit, which is the pace setter for the other runners. I was not a full-time student, so I was not allowed to win points for the team. I was allowed, however, to try and set the pace too high at the beginning of a run, so as to make the opposing team go out too fast, too soon. A highlight of my time on the team was meeting the Golden State Warriors when they were visiting to play an exhibition game.

The Air Force sent me back to Lackland AFB in Texas for the Olympic trials. I had one of the fastest times in the 10K race. However, they placed me in the one-mile category, which was not at all my forte. It seemed quite evident to me that this was a political play of sorts. I had no coach. I was not a full-time student. I had no pedigree so to speak—like so many others coming from affluent colleges. It appeared that I was set up to fail.

In 1967, the first-ever Las Vegas Marathon took place, so I decided to enter it—just for fun. I didn't have any running shoes (of course, designer athletic shoes were not a thing at that time), so I ran in an old pair of Hush Puppies. I will share more about this experience in a later chapter.

Rich and I also began deadheading cars for Avis. When they had too many cars in Vegas, we would deadhead the cars to where they were needed. It was a wild adventure as Nevada had no speed limits back then. So there we were, flying down the highway between Las Vegas and Los Angeles reaching speeds up to 120 mph. It was rather thrilling for two daring, young guys like us. On one such occasion while going full boar, Rich blew a tire. Thankfully, he lived to tell about it. In general, it was an exciting time to be in Las Vegas. All the great legends were playing there: the Rat Pack (Frank Sinatra, Dean Martin, Sammy Davis, Jr., and Joey Bishop), Jerry Lewis, and, of course, Elvis.

A later photo of Gerry with Air Force buddy, Rich Pyles, taken at the wedding reception of son, Mike, and daughter-in-law, Katie, at Planet Hollywood, in Las Vegas.

At that time everyone in the Air Force was getting early outs at three years. Rich got out at three years and one month. But I got orders to go to Thailand. It was 1968. I moved Carol back to Santa Rosa, bought a house in Montgomery Village for about $18,000, and then left for Thailand.

I got stationed far north at NKP (Nakhon Phanom), just across from the DMZ (demilitarized zone) in Vietnam. From NKP, A-1 bombers would bomb the DMZ daily. Years later, I discovered my friend at the phone company, Roger Moore, was also stationed at NKP, but in a different job. I got promoted to staff sergeant (four stripes) while there. NKP was a jungle base and North Vietnam sympathizers were in the area, which meant a five-mile trip into the local village along the Mekong River was always dangerous. We still went into the village every week. We were willing to take the risk just to get away.

Being a radio guy, we bunked and worked close to the flight line. While I was there, a couple of A-1 planes fully loaded with bombs crashed on takeoff. The pilots died. This happened twice. I was stunned—literally, as I suffered concussions and had to lie down for several hours each time to recover.

While at NKP, I made several trips to Bangkok to obtain parts. On one trip, I was asked to go to a Thai base called Kow Yai that was on top of a mountain at a game preserve reserved for the king and queen of Thailand. I had to take a Baht bus (five cent bus) alone from Bangkok. I had to travel quite a ways until I arrived at the game preserve. At the preserve, I was given a jeep and a place to bunk. It was quite an adventure because there were wild elephants and tigers around. I was also warned severely about the two-step snakes—very deadly snakes that if bitten, you supposedly only can take two steps before dying. I did encounter one up close in my time at the preserve, but thankfully, I was able to escape unscathed.

My job at Kow Yai was to teach the Thai military how to fix the American radios they had been given to defend their airplanes. I spent a month there and even helped the Thai army use jackhammers to fix a road. At 135 pounds, I was actually bigger than anyone in the Thai army. The average Thai man is ninety-five pounds. I spoke very little Thai, and they spoke very little English, so we mostly pointed to communicate.

I visited my friend Keith Rohde in Korat before returning to NKP. Then, Butch Walters, a Colorado native I met at NKP, and I volunteered to go to Vietnam to help fix radios. We arrived in Da Nang and were assigned to Monkey Mountain. After being there for a week, a crisis came up on the DMZ (right on the front lines of the war), at Dong Ha. They were supposed to have twenty radio channels available to support helicopters, bombers, and ground troops. They were down to only two channels. The men assigned there were not capable of fixing the communications.

Butch and I volunteered and were there in eighteen hours. We flipped a coin to see who would work the twelve hours of daylight and who would take the nightshift. Between the two of us, we needed to work round the clock in order to get the job done in a timely manner. Of course, I lost the coin toss—I always seemed to. Initially, we worked together for about ten hours and got seven channels back up. Then, we split up, and within one day, we had twelve channels back up. The upside of losing the coin toss and having to work the graveyard shift, was that I was one of the first in line at the chow hall for breakfast. If you were in line early enough, you got fresh eggs. They didn't have an ample supply, so the latecomers had to eat green, powdered eggs. No thank you! We spent several months there and kept the communications working until the site was destroyed in a monsoon.

The two "Butches": Gerry with his friend Lloyd ("Butch") Walters in Bangkok, Thailand. Gerry's family called Gerry "Butch," as it was a common nickname back in the day.

While stationed at Dong Ha, Vietnam, I had to take several trips south to Da Nang to get parts. On one trip, I dropped into the communications center to send my brother, Steve, a message. We were both in the same general vicinity at the same time—me in Vietnam and he on the USS *Oriskany*, just off the coast of Vietnam. We had not seen each other in four years (counting training at school and then being deployed overseas), but the Navy operations center would only allow official business messages to be sent. While I was arguing about wanting to send a message to my brother, the commander overheard me and asked if I had taken my R and R (rest and recuperation—a week off from the war zone). I told him I really couldn't afford a vacation, as I sent all my money home to support my wife and our house payments. The Navy commander said if my commander said it was okay, then I could fly out to the aircraft carrier with him and spend my R and R with my brother on the ship.

I spent ten days on the carrier. Unfortunately for my brother, he spent four years in the Navy and never got to experience taking off from or landing on a carrier flight deck. Because my brother was a cook and often fixed special meals for the chiefs, when the chiefs found out that I was visiting from Vietnam, they gave my brother and I a tour of their different areas of the ship. I was glad that my brother got to see areas of the ship that had previously been off limits to him. All in all, that trip was by far one of the most memorable of my time in the service, and for my brother as well.

Gerry on the USS *Oriskany* visiting his brother, Steve. An unforgettable experience for both of them.

In my time overseas, I witnessed a number of wounded men and at times I was even called upon to give aid to some of them. I was so thankful to never have to endure what many others went through. I'd have to say that aside from the concussions, the only other hazard I suffered was that my hearing was impacted to some degree because of my proximity to the action. Back in those days, we were not provided with any ear protection, and I was constantly exposed to extremely loud noise. At one point, I needed to have a hernia surgery in Cheng Mai, Thailand. The only frightening thing about that experience was when a local nurse prepped me for the operation. She approached me with a razor knife in hand and said in broken English, "I no do before."

Not very reassuring! Thankfully, I made it through the procedure without incident.

All in all, my time in the military was a very valuable experience. I was proud to serve my country, along with my brother, and carry on the family tradition as both my dad and uncle also had served. I was raised in an era when patriotism was high, and the majority of Americans respected the flag, the rule of law, and their freedom. It is sad to think about where we are as a nation today, to see how much of our nation's character we have lost. Although our country was founded on Judeo-Christian principles, we have since lost our way—and I believe that we will pay a high price for turning our backs on God as a result. Of course, at that point in my life I had not discovered God.

While my friends were all getting early outs, I was about to hit four years and was trying to get back to the States. I actually went over four years by just one day. There was a logistical error in being processed out. They couldn't get me out of Vietnam and back home before my four years elapsed. I was pretty upset at the time, as I was anxious to get back home. Then I was told because I had gone one day into my fifth year, I would be receiving an additional thirty days' leave pay as a staff sergeant. When the time finally came to head stateside, I went to Travis Air Force Base to finish getting processed out.

Soon after, I was making repeated trips to take military friends to the San Francisco airport so they could fly home after also getting discharged at Travis AFB. We were greeted with great hostility and anti-war sentiment. We were wearing civilian clothes, but our buzzed haircuts gave us away as having been in the military. This was the second time I was spat upon, and it was very deflating. I had served my country well. I had made sacrifices. There were many times I was in harm's way while in Thailand and Vietnam. I didn't regret a moment of it. I would do it again. But I couldn't believe the utter disrespect I received from people who had no clue about the price of freedom. I understood that not everybody sees the world the same way. However, for those who would argue for peace, not war, disrespecting others and their point of view is not the way to cultivate peace.

For over a year, I had been sending all my pay back home to Carol, and she was supposed to be working, as we had no children yet. When I got home, I found out Carol had decided not to work anymore, and she had used all the money we had saved—all the money I had sent home. I knew my being gone so long must've been hard on her, yet I felt like there had been a major breach in trust. It was the beginning of the disintegration of our marriage.

It was around this same time that I became interested in politics. Back home in Santa Rosa, I ran for city council and then for state assembly in the Eighth District. As part of my campaign ads, I wore a T-shirt I had designed that read Running for State Assembly and which I wore as I continued my training runs through the city streets. I lost my election bid, but I had no regrets entering the race. It was a very educational experience.

Campaign ad: Gerry captured many an onlooker's attention as he ran through the city streets of Santa Rosa while running for City Council. Although he gave the campaign a full effort, he did not finish the race with a win.

At twenty-three years old, I took the first job I could find. Sonoma Engineering and Research made microwave para-amps for Hughes aircraft (for the space program). The pay was minimum wage ($1.75 an hour) with the promise of bonuses and a promotion after three months. Talking with other co-workers there, I soon discovered that many had been there for nine months or a year and had never seen a bonus or promotion. I decided to go to work in San Francisco for the phone company. Within a month, three of the other guys at S.E.R. quit and joined me at Pacific Bell. I worked in the financial district on the telegraph board (yes, we still had the telegraph board in 1969).

Carol and I argued about her not working. That's when it came out that she had also decided she really didn't want any children. My working long hours due to the commute to San Francisco didn't help much either. I was a hard worker and a good provider to Carol, but I had always known that I wanted to have children. The tradeoff ended up being that I would have a vasectomy after she had a baby, much to my great disappointment.

On Christmas Eve, 1971, at twenty-five years old (only two weeks shy of having two years on the job with Pac Bell), my friend Neville Howse and I were returning from work in San Francisco. We stopped at the south end of Santa Rosa so Neville could get a car part before we went home. When he got back in the car, it wouldn't start. It was a stick shift, so we knew we could bump start it. I went to the rear of the car on the right side to push it. While I was pushing, a drunk driver, doing about forty miles per hour, passed a car on the right side, veering into the parking lane. He hit me, crushing me between the bumper and grills of the two cars.

The highway patrol knew where the point of impact was because I was hit so hard that my feet popped out of my laced shoes. My body was found about one hundred and fifty feet down the road. The exhaust pipe of Neville's car went clear through my left knee. The bones in my back, my leg bones, arm bones, and ribs were mostly all broken. I was pronounced dead by the highway patrol and the EMT on the scene. I was also pronounced dead by staff at the hospital. They notified Carol that I had passed. At the time of the accident, Carol was eight months pregnant with our son, Mike.

The hospital required two doctors to sign off on the death certificate. The second doctor decided to pump fluid in me to see if they could detect any heartbeat before signing the certificate. It seemed to work, as I revived with a faint pulse. They needed to get permission to amputate my left leg, if needed, due to the exhaust pipe going through it. However, they decided to hold off on the amputation until I stabilized after a couple of days so as not to shock the body too much. Thankfully, they were able to save my leg.

After many hours of surgery, my body was strapped down to a flat, fixed surface. Due to my back being crushed, paralysis was a strong possibility. This is how I spent the first ten days of recovery. It was an excruciating time not just because of the pain but because of the extreme limitations and uncertainty about the future. I had plates, pins, and screws installed in my left leg and arm. I was told I would never walk again without a limp. Any athletic ambitions I might have had looked bleak.

I had initially been pronounced dead at the scene by the CHP and paramedics and then had been considered to be clinically dead by the first doctor at the hospital, yet I was actually still alive. Since I did not have a relationship with the Lord at that point in time, I gave all the credit to the hospital staff instead of God. In fact, many people have asked me about those first moments after being hit. They asked if I saw any light or tunnel or experienced some glimpse into eternity or not. My response was, "No—just total darkness."

Let me be clear. I don't believe I came back to life because I don't believe I ever actually died. I had such a faint pulse and had lost so much blood that my pulse was undetectable, but I was barely alive. When the hospital staff determined that they would try measures to see if I could be saved, it was a last-ditch effort on their part, and even in those critical hours to follow, I still very easily could have died.

I spent the next two years with casts on my leg and arm. I started out in a wheelchair and eventually went on crutches. My left arm would not heal, so the bone had to be re-broken and recast two more times. I lost the use of my left elbow. After four months of being in casts and while still on crutches, I was told that I would lose my job if I couldn't return to work within the next six months. I got restless and decided to return to work, even in casts. So, I'd hop on the five a.m. bus to San Francisco every morning. I had to sit in an aisle seat due to my casts. When I got my casts off after two years, I resumed jogging again—very slowly at first. Of course, I had to have them surgically remove the plates, screws, and pins from my body, as they were interfering with my running.

Road runner: Gerry made a remarkable comeback from his near-fatal accident. Determined to resume his athletic pursuits, he went on to win many races over the years. Even in 2022, at age seventy-six, he continued to challenge himself.

About a year after I had recovered, the economy was depressed, and I invested in a couple of cheap apartment buildings in town and also a thirty-acre walnut orchard that was in foreclosure in a nearby county. I started spending time working more on the properties. I still wanted more children, but it was a dream no longer possible. At least we had our son, Mike.

The tensions kept mounting as we disagreed on some major issues. Our marriage continued to deteriorate. I became more involved in politics and began attending meetings and conferences, as well as apartment rental work. I would spend time with Mike, but Carol and I ignored each other.

Gerry's green '56 T-bird. He enjoyed cruising in this car and even drove it in a few parades for the Big Brothers/Big Sister's club in Sonoma County, of which he was an active member as a Big Brother.

I was at a meeting in Fairfield when I got a call that Carol had been taken to the hospital due to an aneurysm. She survived but was permanently disabled. During the year Carol spent in a medical facility recovering, I would take Mike to his grandparents during the days and care for him on my off hours and weekends. After a couple of more years, Carol had recovered as best as possible. She couldn't drive, due to vision problems, but was able to care for Mike at home. She was able to call her parents for help, if needed, as they lived only two blocks away.

When our marriage did eventually end, Carol took the house and got custody of Mike. The courts in those days would not separate the mother from the children unless the mother was a criminal. We sold some apartments, and I gave Carol the money. I kept one very old fourplex and the acreage.

During this time, I also managed to complete enough college credits at San Francisco State University at night to finally graduate with a four-year degree in interdisciplinary studies (economics). I applied for graduation, only to find out that, over the years, the requirements to graduate had changed. I needed two college-level English courses. No way! My very worst subject! I was told if I passed a bypass exam, I could still graduate. Otherwise, I would need to complete another year. I decided to take the bypass exam.

The Friday before my test, I felt sick after work and threw up all the way home (and all night too). On Saturday morning, on the way back to the city to take the exam I had to stop twice to throw up some more. When I got to the test site, I had to leave class once to throw up again. At the exam, we were told to write a paper on any subject to earn a pass or fail grade.

I sat there for half the period staring at a blank piece of paper. Then, I remembered how the toilet I had been over most of the night had to flush and fill up—just like an electric capacitor charging and discharging. In that moment, I had an epiphany and realized I could write about the toilet and capacitor analogy. So I did, and, lo and behold, I passed the exam and graduated! I still didn't recognize that God may have had a role in keeping me over a toilet all night. God, the Bible, and church were not yet a part of my life.

I went on to begin pursuing a master's degree at UC Berkeley. My life was full of responsibilities, but I was always driven to learn more, achieve more, and do more. I took only one class a semester, plus a summer school class, so I knew it would take a while, but it was worth the effort. Even though I eventually completed the general course requirements, it was considered a short course masters: no thesis, so no actual degree.

My parents were largely responsible for instilling in my brother and me the importance of getting a good college education. My brother was the genius. Yet I was the one who had the desire to pursue higher education. In many ways, it seemed not to serve me well. The secular teaching I received took me farther away from an understanding of God and what really mattered most in life. I was on this quest to achieve and to push myself to greater heights. My priorities were wrong, and I never felt fulfilled. How could I? I had not yet discovered my life's purpose.

Meanwhile, I had been spending much of my free time working on my walnut orchard. It had a barn and a well but no house. I thought maybe I would move there when I retired. It was a foreclosure, and I got it really cheap. Within a few years, I got transferred to Ukiah, so I decided to build a home on the property as it was only twenty-five minutes from my job. This was during the economic downturn in California, when the majority of contractors and builders were out of work. I found two contractors who were willing to help me build the house for the cost of materials and ten dollars an hour each for labor. A year later, I had a beautiful home.

During that time, I reconnected with an old high school acquaintance. We both were struggling with the disappointment of our failed marriages and facing the challenges of a new reality. As is common in many rebound relationships, we got married a short time later. She had custody of her two daughters, and we tried to build a family together.

We had to live in a travel trailer and a camper while the house was being built at the orchard. We also bought a twenty-two-foot Sea Ray boat and began water skiing on weekends. Eventually, I learned to slalom.

One of my greatest joys, however, was not in recreational activities but in working on projects with Mike. When he was in his early teens, my Temple Street apartment units were in need of some serious renovations. It was a great opportunity to spend some father-son time together while teaching him some very useful skills. I would schedule remodeling projects, and I would travel down to Santa Rosa once a month to work with him on making the improvements. We tore down walls, worked on plumbing and electrical projects, replaced claw-foot tubs with modern tubs, replaced windows and doors, and tore up floors, as needed. Even though this went on for a year and a half, that time spent with Mike was well worth the effort and one of the most memorable times in my life. During this time, I purchased an old Willy's camo jeep. Mike and I stripped it to the bones and rebuilt it from scratch. With Mike approaching driving age in just a few short years, I wanted him to understand the basic workings of a vehicle and to become adept at tinkering and doing his own repairs. Ironically, the vehicles he later came to own were nearly impossible to maintain on his own. But no regrets. Along the way, the skills proved very helpful with some of the trucks he owned in his late teens and early adult years.

Sadly, even with having a family, a good job, a nice house, a dog, and a boat, I began wondering what was missing from my life. I was not fulfilled. I felt empty. Just a few years into my second marriage, I filed for divorce. I had failed . . . again. In the course of the break-up, we lost the property, as we couldn't make payments with the new house on it. I also sold the fourplex in Santa Rosa to settle our affairs.

There I was—single, with no bills, but also no money. Mike, who was almost fourteen at the time, was understandably impacted by my two divorces. Not to mention I was working all the time and living two counties away from him.

In the midst of all this, I met Monica, who worked in the Ukiah central office. She had two young daughters (ages three and six years old). I was thirty-eight, and she was twenty-six. We became fast friends and enjoyed talking about deep matters in life. We began to date. She was a born-again believer, so as a result of our growing relationship, I actually began going to church regularly for the first time in my life. I started to open a Bible and read it with great interest.

After a time, we married at the home of one of the couples from our church. At that point in my life, I realized I had been deceived by the world. I began to realize that this life was not primarily about jobs, money, or education but about finding a relationship with God. Previously, I had placed a high priority on education and was always very driven—a self-professed workaholic. Even though I had previously enjoyed pleasures like boating and taking vacations, I knew they didn't truly satisfy. Up until then, I had not fully understood my purpose in life.

So, I professed Jesus as my Lord and Savior—a decision I wish I had made long before.

A Kodak moment–Four generations of Burney men: Gerry's Grandpa Quay, Gerald Sr., Steve, and Gerry (holding young Mike).

A younger version of Gerry and Monica on a carriage ride through Central Park, New York.

37

California cruisin': Many road trips were taken in this Porsche 914, primarily to bike races all over Northern California. The car covered piles of miles and took Gerry and Monica to some very obscure and interesting places.

Gerry, Monica, Vanessa, and Hillary at a family Thanksgiving gathering in Sacramento.

Family portrait, circa the late 1990s.

As Monica and I continued to mature in our Christian lives, we desired to create a Christ-centered home. To be specific, we wanted more than just to attend church on Sundays. Rather, we wanted to be involved in kingdom work to the glory of God. The girls were both still young, and so we decided that Monica would quit work and be more available at home. By this time, Mike (who still lived in Santa Rosa with Carol) was getting older and becoming busier with school activities. We were able to spend time with him on a few weekends a month and attended his band concerts and track meets. We would reach out to Mike as much as possible, but at times, were hindered by distance and schedules.

Although I was thankful for a job that provided comfortably for our family, I was not necessarily passionate about my career. In my first year, I worked with two guys who were both about to retire and leave me alone with the entire area. Working in microwave radio was a good job, and I had many unexpected adventures.

My first winter there was a violent snow and windstorm on Cahto Peak. At five thousand feet, the wind and snow were clocked at ninety miles per hour at times. On one occasion, one of the antennae covers actually blew off and bent the feed horn, isolating the coastal areas from the interior of Mendocino County. Jerry (one of the older guys who was close to retiring) and I responded to the situation in a Sno-Cat. Being older, Jerry stayed on the ground while I climbed the tower in the middle of the snowstorm. Winds were dangerously high. There was no safety net and no safety harness—just the grip of my hands in the frigid cold.

The plan was to lasso the feed horn with the rope. Then together we would pull on the rope and hopefully bend the feed horn back into place to restore service. It took me three trips up the tower. I had to come down to get warm and then I would try again. On the third attempt, I finally succeeded in lassoing the feed horn. I brought the rope down to where Jerry was. Once back on the ground, he and I put our full weight into pulling the feed horn back. After six hours, the communications were restored between the coast and inland.

Often in my specialized job, in the midst of severe storms I would be called out in the night to respond alone to a failure at a microwave repeater site. I would have to travel a distance to reach repeater sites at the top of area mountain ranges (elevations upwards of six thousand feet). In high winds, rain, snow—at all hours of the night—off I'd go. It reminded me of the unofficial creed of the United States Post Office mail carriers: "Neither snow nor rain nor heat nor gloom of night stays these couriers from the swift completion of their appointed rounds."

Microwave radio tower at one of many sites Gerry maintained as a craft person with the phone company. After hanging up his tools, he became a manager in microwave radio. His territory spanned the Bay Area to the Oregon border.

Modes of transportation: Gerry was asked to drive a Sno-Cat up to the Sierras for a phone company school. His only task was to deliver the Sno-Cat. After the mission was accomplished, he took the opportunity to challenge himself up at high elevation in preparation for the upcoming racing season.

In addition to the challenge of having to travel to remote locations alone in the night in storms, sometimes my company vehicle would not always make it to the top due to deep snow or downed trees. It was not at all uncommon in the winter for me to have to hike into a site with snowshoes, often encountering fresh bear tracks and evidence of other wild animals nearby. And, in the warmer months, I'd pass through heavily guarded pot farms, met by the watchful eye of growers. The key was to make my presence known by being as noisy as possible and passing through their territory as quickly as possible. My well-marked company vehicle also helped diffuse any concern about my being an unwelcome intruder, as well.

Another time, Larry, my good friend Roger, and I had to repair a trouble at Cahto Peak (which is between Laytonville and Fort Bragg). After we got things running again, we were making our way down the hill when the left track clutch failed, forcing the Sno-Cat off the path and down the mountain. Roger was hanging off the back end since the cab accommodated only two people. As the Cat went off of a snowy cliff, Roger bailed, and Larry and I ended up tumbling inside the cab down the steep hill. Larry, being elderly, ended up pretty banged up, with multiple cuts and bruises. I was a little banged up, but the worst of it for me was a hole in my jeans from some spilled battery acid. Roger caught up with us once the Cat came to its resting place. We were far enough down the hill at that point to be rescued by a vehicle, so Roger stayed with Larry while I ran about a mile and a half down to where our vehicle was parked. As harrowing an experience as it was, we were thankful to make it out alive, as we knew it could very easily have ended a whole lot worse.

I would never complain about my thirty-three years working at the phone company. It allowed me to be a good provider for my family. I did have to work a lot of overtime due to the specific nature of my field, which took precious time away from the family. But I never intentionally sought opportunities to work extra hours. I was glad that I finally learned that making money was not the key to fulfillment. My job was just a job to me—a means to an end. I'm glad my background early on had led to my having a secure job with good benefits, but I wouldn't at all say that it was my calling in life.

Over time, as I grew in my understanding of God, I did become more and more passionate about serving Him and about understanding and sharing His Word with others. My first ministry assignment was working with the young boys in our church once a week. We would build various small projects. The first project they made was a toolbox. After that with each completed service project to bless others (like flower boxes and birdhouses), they would earn a tool for their toolbox.

I was then asked to be the youth director and work with the older youth, leading them in Bible studies. At that time, some annual events were being established at our church: The Trinity 500 (soap box derby), the Climb for Christ Bike Challenge, and a kite fly. It was a good time for the young, and the young at heart joined in the fun, cheering on the former. I also took our youth group, with a couple of other chaperones, to the state youth conference over the holidays several years in a row.

On one particular trip, one of the chaperones got drunk one evening at the bar at the hotel where we were staying. Even though it was difficult to have to explain to the kids (and especially to the parents when we returned home), it was not entirely in vain, as it provided a teachable moment. We were able to talk to the kids about trust, God's mercy and forgiveness, and praying for the person who erred. I explained to them that we can forgive the person, but that he could not be trusted working with youth again, at least not until he had earned back the leaders' trust. I shared how God is patient with us and will forgive us when we ask Him for forgiveness when we blow it. To be truly forgiven, however, a sincerely repentant heart cannot continue to repeat their sin.

Eventually, God called us to another church in a neighboring town. By that time, Monica and I had started to attend classes through the distant learning Southern Baptist seminary extension program out of Nashville. Our area director of missions, Jim Murcray, was our first instructor. Over the course of seven years, we had two other instructors who were local pastors and friends of ours. I had even begun filling in at the pulpit for area pastors on occasion, as the need arose.

In the early days of being at our new church, we offered a movie ministry to the youth in the community. Since it was a very small, rural community, there wasn't much for kids to do on weekends, except perhaps to get into trouble, so we had a pretty sizeable turnout. We would have good discussions after the movies. Some of the kids came to know the Lord through this ministry and were baptized. It was meeting a need and was so encouraging to see the fruit God brought forth from it.

THE AGE OF BECOMING

One older high school boy (who happened to be the pastor's son) was beginning to struggle with his faith. He was not able to understand, for example, how an innocent baby could be born a sinner. He was grappling with a lot of the same questions I had had over time. By that point in my life, I saw value in answering questions like that in a clear, concise way, knowing that many others would also be looking for explanations to their conundrums.

Around the same time our daughters were receiving some humanist teachings at school, and I wanted to keep them on the right path and help them be able to defend their faith. So God directed me to write a pocket-sized pamphlet that addressed these concerns from a biblical worldview. Over time, it grew into a book-length project. Over many more years, I split the book into five different books (see www.targettruthministries.com). How ironic that God would have this remedial English student go on to pen several books—and actually enjoy writing them!

About midway through our time at that church, the pastor moved away, and I was asked to be the interim pastor. After a short period of time, I was called and licensed into the ministry. This occurred toward the end of my career working at the phone company. After several years had passed, God called us back to our first church, in Ukiah. I served as associate pastor there for several years. It was there that I was ordained as a minister of the gospel.

Before I retired from the phone company, I obtained my teaching credential and got a job at a Christian school. Just prior to beginning to teach, I developed an ear infection on top of my already bad hearing from Vietnam, and that turned into permanent hearing loss. It became problematic in communicating with the kids in the class, so I had to quit after just one year. I substituted here and there through the public schools for a while afterward, because there was such a need for substitutes, and I needed to supplement my retirement income. I also took on a few other jobs—at a mill and as a truck driver.

By this time, I had been filling in for a fellow pastor at the jail, leading Bible studies. It was quite evident that our local jail would greatly benefit from having a chaplain, as people who had loved ones at the jail (like a grandmother attending our former church, whose grandson was incarcerated) were having trouble getting into the jail for a visit. Even pastors had trouble getting in to see inmates. There also had been a number of suicides over the years among the inmates, as well.

Someone suggested I approach the sheriff about developing a chaplaincy at the jail. I prayed about it and felt God was leading me to begin the process of becoming the first-ever chaplain at the Mendocino County Jail and Juvenile Hall. Initially, I went through the Good News Prison Ministry, which is headquartered out of Richmond, Virginia. It is a nationwide ministry that helps communities develop a chaplaincy program at their local jail. The daughter of the founder of the ministry flew out twice to help me get started. However, the Good News ministry has certain criteria that had to be met in order for them to be involved. A certain level of income must be guaranteed through supporting churches in a given county. Sarah traveled all around Mendocino County, meeting with pastors at various churches. She secured a commitment from more than several churches, but when she came back a few months later, things had changed. The amount of support needed to sustain the chaplaincy was not there. All she could offer me was to provide a week's training at their headquarters in Richmond.

I went to the training, and it was very helpful. I also met with a chaplain at a jail in the Bay Area. Through the support of some of the churches, as well as a number of individuals, I was able to establish the chaplaincy. We could cover ministry needs but no salary. Since I had additional retirement income, I could get by just fine. The caveat with the Good News Prison Ministry was that if I were to have to step down from the chaplaincy at some point and a younger person stepped into that role with a young family to support, there needed to be a certain fixed income in place. The goal was to ensure that the chaplaincy would continue no matter who filled the position.

Since our county jail had never had a chaplain before, the powers that be devised stringent requirements. The chaplain had to have: (1) a four-year college degree, (2) one year's experience as a psychologist, counselor, or have a teaching credential (with one year's teaching experience), (3) been in the military or worked one year as a sheriff's deputy or police officer, (4) attended seminary, and (5) served a year as an ordained pastor in a nationally recognized denomination. That was a tall order, but not to God. Little did they know that God had set in place stepping-stones along the way to prepare me for this role. I checked all their boxes, jumped through all the necessary hoops and was approved. I had gone to college but for most of my years since, I never had a use for my degree—until then. Go figure!

Within the first year as a jail chaplain, Hugo Boeckx, the inmate service coordinator who helped advocate for getting me into the jail chaplaincy, passed away from cancer. In that early time of my jail ministry, I was met with resistance by some of the deputies and inmates. I was even spat upon by a few of the inmates. As a general rule, I'm not one to take things personally. I knew they were really rejecting God and not me. Getting spat upon when returning from Vietnam was far more offensive to me. Representing Christ to the lost leaves believers open to all forms of persecution. We are told to expect it and to embrace it as part of being a Christ-follower (see Phil. 1:29).

During that time, our oldest daughter, Vanessa, was getting married in Italy and asked me to officiate the ceremony. Not being much of a traveler, I had no real interest in going to Europe, aside from the wedding. Monica, however, enjoys traveling, and I knew it was a great opportunity for her to see the sites and experience a different culture. Thinking it might be our only trip abroad, I decided to extend the trip and see more of Europe while we were there. Little did we know at the time, that our younger daughter, Hillary, would later be called to serve the Lord as a long-term missionary in Sicily!

Since I was still new to the chaplaincy, I was concerned about how I was going to care for the inmates while we were away. God impressed upon me to write weekly sermon messages I called Virtual Chapels. They also contained a cartoon and had some little word puzzles for their enjoyment. When we returned, the weekly messages were so well received, the inmates requested that I keep them coming. As of this writing, sixteen years later,

I have written over hundreds of Virtual Chapels and continue to write them.

The amazing thing, though, is how God's ways truly are higher and better than our ways (see Isa. 55:9). Maybe it shouldn't have been a surprise when the inmates wanted me to keep writing and delivering these messages to them weekly as God assures us that His Word does not return to Him void (see Isa. 55:11). Not only did I see this verse come to life as I began to see lives being transformed at the local jail, but God had an even broader plan in mind.

There are eight sections to our jail. Some people are in the unsentenced sections, others are in the sentenced sections. Once someone has been sentenced, at some point many are sent off to prison elsewhere around the country. As some of these inmates got shipped off to prison, they requested that I keep sending them the Virtual Chapels. The mailing list started to grow exponentially—and not just with inmates I ministered to at our local jail. I also started receiving requests to be added to our mailing list from prisoners who received the Virtual Chapels from their cellies (cellmates). I was now corresponding with people whom I had never even met!

Through our Target Truth Ministries, my wife and I have been able to send the Virtual Chapels monthly and once a year send my books to these prisoners at other facilities, in addition to supplying books for the bookshelves in the different sections of our jail. We also often have had inmates request Bibles and other books. It is only through the generous financial gifts of our faithful supporters that we have had the means to accommodate their requests. Just to be clear, even though I was the only chaplain at our jail, and the only one who actually went into the jail over those sixteen years and met with the inmates directly at their cell, my wife was and still is very much a part of our jail and prison ministry. She partners with me in prayer, had accompanied me at times when a female inmate got out of jail and needed our support, and still helps with the massive paperwork involved with the monthly mailings. For several years, we also had a small army of women from our church helping us with the mailings.

For many years at Christmastime, our dear friend Pastor Donnell organized several churches (including our own) to assemble gift bags for the inmates. These decorated bags included six hand-baked cookies, seven pieces of candy, a Christian tract, a pocket calendar, and three Christmas cards with postage on them to send to their loved ones. Sadly, because the Covid pandemic has changed the protocol on so many things, we haven't been able to give these expressions of God's love to the inmates, except for the cards. The cards and cookies have been especially meaningful to them over the years, as they have appreciated being able to send a message to their families, and some had never had homemade cookies before. (Groups like the Gideons and Bible study leaders had also previously been able to meet with a small number of inmates for Bible studies until the pandemic hit.)

The support for the inmates has come in other forms as well. Our local bike shop often receives abandoned or donated broken-down bikes. They refurbish them and give them to us to pass on to inmates in need of transportation whey they get out of jail. Whenever I can, I also pass along bikes to those in need at the Center for Hope, our local Christian homeless day center where I volunteer sharing a devotional with the guests a few days a week. The bikes help them get around town more easily.

The phenomenal success of our ministries must be attributed in large part to the faithful prayers from those who support us. One such prayer warrior, our dear friend Shasta, recently went home to be with the Lord. At ninety-five years old, she made such a tremendous impact on our ministries through her prayers, financial support, and words of encouragement. In her later years, she struggled with various health issues and was almost entirely homebound. She would get so discouraged and felt useless to God because of her limitations. She longed to be out of her suffering and looked forward to her forever home in heaven. We would often try to encourage her and let her know that she was a crucial part of God's kingdom work through our ministries. Her prayers, as well as her financial gifts, made it possible for countless Virtual Chapels to make their way all across the country, radically changing hearts and lives forever.

Many churches and individuals have answered our request for books, devotional materials, and magazines to give to the local inmates. One of the distinguishing things about the time spent with Sarah from Good News Prison Ministries is that she shared that she travels all around the country and has seen the inside of many jails. She commented that Mendocino County Jail is by far one of the worst facilities she had ever seen. It actually happens to be one of the oldest jails in California. There is no gymnasium to hold chapel services, and the only meeting room is a former mattress storage room that holds up to only ten people at a time for Bible studies. When the room is in use, attorneys often have to meet in the hallway, with no privacy. There has been talk for a number of years of building a new facility, but for now, it's just that—talk.

Interestingly though, one inmate that came through our jail a number of years ago was transferred to Lake County (the next county over from us to the east). They have a gymnasium where they hold chapel services weekly. Yet, he wrote a letter to us requesting to still receive the Virtual Chapels. They were far more effective because the chapel services where he was were very brief and repetitive. Whereas the Virtual Chapels were a useful Bible study tool since they contain many Scripture verses and could be revisited time and again. How ironic that bigger and newer isn't necessarily better.

We have been blessed to receive numerous letters over the years—mostly expressing gratitude, and some containing beautiful artwork done in pencil. I never set out to serve God for any rewards I might receive (temporal or eternal) but receiving hand-drawn pictures and hearing the stories of how God has taken broken, messed up lives and so dramatically transformed them has been a reward beyond measure. That God would choose to use me as a vessel to carry His Word of truth and hope, when I am so undeserving, continues to amaze and humble me.

My heart has been burdened for those who are despised, many who despise themselves—filled with rage, hopelessness, emptiness. When I met with inmates, I often would ask them, "When you and I are sitting here across from each other, what do you think God sees? Do you think he sees a pastor in a shirt and jeans and you in your orange jumpsuit? Do you think he sees a saint and a sinner? No!" I tell them. "He sees two people who both need the Savior. Without God's grace, mercy, and love, we are eternally lost in our sins and separated from our Creator." It's astounding to see the countenance of these men change when they first hear that message. It's humbling to see their very lives changed by the revelation that no matter what they've done, where they've been, who they've hurt, how much they are hurting, there is hope of redemption.

It has been such a tremendous privilege to be a part of God's beautiful plan all these many years. Not only have many inmates come into a saving relationship with Jesus and wayward believers have been restored to a deeper faith in Him through these messages and books, but families have been healed and jail staff members have been encouraged, all by the light of God's love penetrating the deepest abyss of despair and the hardest of hearts.

So many people on the outside assume that all people in jail are evil. The truth of the matter is that even though there are some very wicked people in the jail, not everyone there is rotten to the core. Not to excuse any wrong acts or behavior, a lot of people in jail just made some really bad choices, took some really wrong turns, or were influenced by the wrong set of people. Getting to know some of the inmates and their back stories has made me realize that though their crime is inexcusable, there often is a cause and effect that explains the why of their behavior or actions. It gives me a godly compassion to help me see them as God sees them and to want to help them see themselves as God sees them. This mindset only helps me to redirect them so that when they do get out of prison, they are not likely to repeat their crimes. I want to see them realize their potential and fulfill their God-given purpose in life.

There was one inmate Pastor Dave Donnell and I mentored for several years. Before being sent off to prison, this once-wretched man who the enemy used for evil purposes was changed into an instrument for righteous purposes. He was in love with the Lord, became a serious student of the Bible, was ordained, and was given the extraordinary assignment of ministering in a unique, wide-open mission field—prison!

Another fellow I know is very earnest about his Christian faith. Even though he has not yet overcome his temptations and continues to struggle with sin patterns in his life, I have spent many years ministering to this brother. I am convinced, without a doubt, that he knows and loves the Lord. He tells people about Jesus all the time. But just like my wife's first stepdad, who never could quite conquer his battle with the bottle, this man undoubtedly has been born again—a sinner, yet a sinner saved by grace. So many believers earnestly believe, but they are weak and because of their lack of self-control, they miss out on many of the blessings God intended for them.

Earlier in the book, I mentioned a young man from our previous church who was disillusioned about the Bible and had trouble grasping some of the main tenets of the faith, such as original sin. Years later, this man (now in his late thirties), after traveling to Hawaii and parts unknown, ended up in our county jail and was in very bad shape. He had developed schizophrenia and had really lost his way. Monica wanted to encourage him by sharing with him that God had used his struggles about Christianity to inspire me to explore my own questions about the Bible. (It was those conversations with that young man that spurred me to write that first apologetic work which grew into five books.) My wife wanted him to know that God had a purpose for his life and that even when we doubt God, even challenge God's intentions and His plan for our lives, we can still be used for kingdom purposes. She wanted him to know no matter where he was in life or what he believed, God still loved him.

Success stories in ministry life can be defined in different ways. Like so many I had counseled with over the years, another guy had been in and out of prison, was often homeless, and with no clear direction for his life. Well, he actually accepted my invitation to come to our church. He annoyed everyone. He talked incessantly, and it was hard to have a conversation with him. He was needy and very much in need of a relationship with Jesus. Thankfully, I was a patient person and was able to befriend this man. Early on in working with inmates and the homeless, I learned how to draw boundaries with people who otherwise would have dominated all my time. Over time, he calmed down and wasn't quite so needy. By listening to him, caring about him, and explaining to him that always dominating conversations is not the best way to endear yourself to people, he learned that to truly communicate with people and build healthy relationships, he needed to listen and not just talk. Despite his character flaws that had repelled many people, he had a compassionate heart.

There was a woman who also had been in and out of jail and was homeless. She was in her thirties but had the mind of a child. She was easily taken advantage of by others, especially men. My caring friend could not stand to see her constantly abused and pilfered out of her monthly government check. He asked her to marry him because he wanted to protect her from those who were using her for their own selfish purposes. She said yes, and I officiated the ceremony. Sadly, it wasn't too long after they were married that she got pulled back to the very people who were seeking to harm her. It broke his heart, but he loved her. It reminded me of the story of Hosea and Gomer. The Israelites were prostituting themselves with other gods. God instructed the prophet Hosea to marry Gomer, a prostitute, as a living illustration to the Israelites of their wickedness (see Hos. 1-3). My friend learned what it was like to love someone wholeheartedly, to be faithful to them, and to want the very best for their life. Yet there is betrayal, unfaithfulness, and heartache. Eventually, she left him, and not long afterward, he passed from heart failure.

I am so thankful I met this man. He was someone who really touched my life. When he lay in the hospital dying, he left a message on our voice mail that said how grateful he was to have known Monica and me. He wanted us to know he loved us and how we had made a huge difference in his life. I wish things had gone better for him over the span of his life, and though I was sad to lose this friend, I was at peace since he left this world knowing that he was loved and redeemed by His Creator and that he had friends that dearly loved him.

Another inmate who became special to me was a man who struggled profoundly with alcohol. As with so many, it completely changed the trajectory of his life. He had previously had a wife, a house, and a steady job at a well-established company in town. But his need for alcohol surpassed his need for self-respect and security. After his wife left him and he lost his job, he soon became homeless. As a result of the alcohol and living on the streets, he developed some serious health problems that put enough scare into him that he entered a rehab program out of the area. I'm happy to say he is doing much better now. He calls me frequently and has expressed how thankful he is to have someone who has encouraged him and been there for him in many different ways. It is always so humbling for me to know that God is using me to help others, even though I am keenly aware of my own imperfections and failings.

Randy (not his real name) was deaf from birth. I have known this man for over thirty years. His primary goal in life is just to survive all the injustices he has suffered. He has lived on the streets for many years. He is another one who is vulnerable and whom people take great advantage. He has ended up in jail from time to time only because he tried to fight back when people have done cruel things to him. One rainy night in the dead of winter, someone came along and burned his backpack containing his meager belongings. Monica and I came across him and found him very distraught. He was so discouraged; he didn't even have a dry pair of socks. We went to a nearby store and bought him several pairs of socks and prayed with him. I wish we could've done more, but we did what we could do at the time. It reminded me of James 2:16-18. It is not enough to say to someone who has a desperate practical need, "I'll pray for you—be well." True compassion requires us to sacrifice of ourselves.

Monica and I have lived a blessed life. We try to share what we can, as often as we can, but we can't help everyone. We certainly can't save anyone—only Jesus saves. However, just like Peter in Acts 3:6, we can say, "Silver and gold I do not have, but what I have I give you." We can share the hope that we have in Jesus Christ by faith. We may not heal anyone of their physical infirmities or help them out of their poverty, but we can testify to the goodness of God and His beautiful gift of salvation for those who would receive it.

I could easily write volumes on all the many more stories of people I've met along the way in the jail, through prison correspondence, and the homeless ministry, of which I have been so honored to be a part. However, I hope sharing just some of the stories has been an encouragement to you to know that God is still in the business of using flawed humans (like myself) to deliver the Good News of His love, mercy, grace, and hope. I hope that you also are encouraged to know that no one is beyond His reach—no matter how hardened is their heart, how wounded they are, or how much they've hurt others. First Peter 4:8 admonishes us to, "Love each other deeply, because love covers over a multitude of sins" (NIV). The greatest commandments we are given are to, "Love the LORD your God with all your heart and with all your soul and with all your mind and with all your strength.' The second is this: 'Love your neighbor as yourself' " (Mark 12:30-31). When we love others with the love of Jesus, miracles happen. Lives are transformed. Love reigns supreme.

THE LETTERS

The following are excerpts from just a mere smattering of the many letters we have received over the past sixteen plus years, both from our local county jail and prison facilities nationwide. I hope these letters will bless you as they have blessed Monica and me. Although I am no longer able to physically go into the jail, a number of inmates have requested to remain on our mailing list for Virtual Chapels and books. We will also continue to send mailings to prisoners all over the country. I was disappointed to have to step down from the jail ministry due to severe hearing loss, but I am thankful knowing that God has brought others forward to minister to the inmates in varying forms.

One such person, our dear friend Gayle, has gone into the women's side of the jail to do Bible studies over the years. She has also been ministering to the youth at Juvenile Hall on Sunday mornings for decades. Several other faithful women have been sharing the load with Gayle, ministering to the women through leading Bible studies. Two faithful men have led Bible studies for Hispanic men, and the Gideons (www.gideons.org) have also been able to take New Testament Bibles into the jail.

In addition to Gayle being approved as one member of a team of chaplains (previously, I was the only chaplain for over sixteen years), our friend Tony is also part of this team and is now leading three Celebrate Recovery groups at the jail each week. I have no doubt whatsoever that God will continue to work amazing miracles through shining the light of His love in the midst of dark places.

It astounds me that God would shower me with so many highly impactful letters of affirmation, since my only desire was to be a "mailman" to deliver His letters of love to inmates and prisoners. More than that, however, it humbles me that God would choose to use such an imperfect man as a vessel of His grace and goodness. Much like the Apostle Paul who saw himself as "the chief of all sinners" (see 1 Tim. 1:15), an inmate once said of himself: "God is using the lowest of the low, to bring glory to the Highest of the High. May He, the only One who is worthy, receive all praise, glory and honor due His holy name." I so identify with this mindset, as it's not about us (see Ps. 115:1). Rather, it's all about Him.

And now, the letters . . .

Pastor Gerry: I am blessed to be allowed to pay for my crimes by serving time . . . yes, blessed. I am totally free in Christ now . . .

The judicial system of California does not love me, but Jesus does!

The judicial system of California does not have mercy on me, but Jesus does!

The judicial system of California does not forgive me, but Jesus does!

The judicial system of California does not bring me peace, but Jesus does!

I have messed up this life, but I will not mess up the prospects of the next one, and there will be a next one!

I hope to hear from you and further my walk with Jesus with your ministry.

(from a state prison in Ione, California)

Chaplain Gerry: I just graduated from 40 days of purpose [program], and I'm now a facilitator for [the] conflict resolution options program. I also finished reading your book on Genesis for the third time. It seems like every time I read it, I get a new perspective—kind of like reading the Bible. I use your material from the book, and the chapel messages, to help others, just like they have helped me. Even in a place like this where there is so much hatred and anger, and violence, it never ceases to amaze me how God can bring light to my life, and cause love to come out of me. I would like to get one of your other books and expand my resources.

(from a state prison in Susanville, California)

Dear Pastor Gerry: I don't have [any] where to go when I get out except the streets, and that will just get me in trouble again, and back to prison. I prayed and asked God what I should do, and then I got celled up with this Christian . . . and he told me about you and the Virtual Chapels. I really thank you so much for all you have done for me since then. I'm so sick of going in and out of jail and prison. I really need to change my life in a positive way, and I know God is the way. I now read the Bible and pray every day, and I'm keeping faith. I would like you to baptize me when I get out.

(from San Quentin Prison, California)

Pastor Gerry: Thank you very much for the newsletters and the book most recently, even though you have never met me. As for God, I never *knew* Him. I am getting to know God now. I believe a big part of my problems in life is that I never knew God, and never even loved myself. I really am trying very hard to give it all to God. I'm getting there. Because of my crime, I'm finally getting to know God and myself. I'm only sorry that my family had to be hurt in the process. On the outside, I had everything—good job, money, a loving family, a good life. But I didn't know God, and all this has been stripped from me because of my crime. My family is standing by me, but we will be separated for many, many years. This has all been humbling, and I cannot tell you how much love this horrible experience has brought forth. It feels as though there is really an Angel from God helping me deal with all this. Please keep the Virtual Chapels coming here. I do so appreciate you keeping me and my family in your prayers. I thank you very much.

(from a California prison)

Pastor Gerry: How are you doin' bro? I want to thank you for sending my wife a copy of your book. She assured me she'll read it. I can't bend her ear like I think you can. I think your books should go national. I found them so easy to read, but it left me hungry for more. . . The fellows here and I use your Virtual Chapels as study guides, as I've saved all the ones that you have sent me. We're loving them like nobody's business. I share all you send me. None of it goes on a shelf . . . Thank you again, pastor.

(from Corcoran Prison, California)

To my brother in Christ: My wife decided to break up with me. I have read all three of the available books here in prison that you have written, and they have reconciled all my questions that I had about God and the Bible. I recognize now that I was not pleasing Christ in my life. I have now accepted the fact that life as I knew it is over, yet I will miss living with my son. I have actually grown thankful of the situation because it led me to Jesus, your books, and to your ministry at the jail. . . . . The prospect of joining in ministry someday has me more excited than I have ever been. Your book on science and origins has helped me understand many confusing issues in life. For this I am forever grateful. I have already begun to use the knowledge I have gained with the help of the Holy Spirit to convince others that the creation story in the Bible is true. . . . I realize that God is using this time in my life to draw me closer to Him. The Bible is my source that eases the pain of being separated from my son. May the grace of our Lord Jesus Christ be with you, my brother—Amen.

(from Folsom Prison, California)

Dear Pastor Gerry: My life is truly changed, all because of Christ. I used to do drugs and drink to cope. I used to depend on what I thought were friends . . . they were, as long as you gave them cash or drugs, etc. Now I know Jesus, and I also know I need to stay away from the world's ways. When I do get out, I plan on being involved in church, and maybe helping others overcome drugs and that lifestyle. I will need friends who love the Lord, so I won't get sidetracked. Thank you so much for your Virtual Chapels and the book you just sent me. God speed.

(from Corona Women's Prison, California)

Pastor Gerry: Thank you for staying in touch with me. And thanks for the new Virtual Chapels and the new book. I read the last book you sent me about three times, and now I lend it out to other men here. Your books have really helped me answer many questions I have always had, and they help me work with other men here, too. The unit here has now put me in charge of organizing the church services, and we have grown from about 10 to over 40 now. I'm doing some singing as well, with our worship group . . . so please pray for me in doing these things. I want to help others have a personal relationship with God and acquire a positive path in this life. I'll stay in touch . . . so I can get involved in ministry somehow. God bless.

(from Susanville State Prison, California)

Pastor Gerry: I hope and pray this letter finds you doing well. I recently came across an issue of your weekly Virtual Chapel that another inmate here gets. I am involved in the prison newspaper here and would like your permission to print parts of your chapel messages in the newspaper. . . . I believe your messages would be a blessing to our audience. Looking forward to hearing from you soon. May the Lord bless you and all those who help support you.

(from Ione Prison, California)

Dear Pastor Burney: I really like the newsletters called the Virtual Chapels that you send to a couple of other inmates here and wonder if you can add me to your mailing list? I also understand from others here that you send a book out to inmates once a year, and if you can, could you send me the one on science and origins. I've always struggled with what I learned in school about the Bible being a myth, and God being a joke. When I was a boy, I had no problem believing that there was a God, but it all seemed so out of place in school with the billions of years and all the facts that science has that there is no need for God. I just decided that I didn't need anyone telling me what was right and wrong, 'cause I am a miracle of stardust and can do whatever seems good to me. Reading your Virtual Chapels has shown me that the prophecies in the Bible really mean there is a God, cause no man could ever foretell that stuff, and your writing on science and stuff showed me how out of touch we all are when we trust what the teachers in school teach us about evolution . . . anyway, thanks in advance.

(from Lake County Jail, California)

Pastor Burney: Let me thank you for staying with me. What I mean is your "mailings" are like a reminder to stay the course and not waver. I had a great job, a great family, and was on top of the world. I really blew it . . . a classic story of selling my soul to the devil. I felt so much guilt and unworthiness that I didn't even go back to church . . . not even here in prison. After my incarceration, because of your Virtual Chapels, I'm back in church, and I'm studying the Bible. The challenge now is believing I am forgiven. I really screwed up out there and I have been totally cut off by my old "Christian" friends and co-workers. But I've come to realize that those I knew probably won't ever forgive me, but Jesus does. I understand the devil's tools of guilt and shame, so I thank you for keeping in touch with me... I really admire your dedication and please keep the Virtual Chapels coming . . . take care and thanks again.

(from Chowchilla Prison, California)

Pastor Gerry: I am still on my quest to seek God with all of my heart and soul. I really love God, Pastor Gerry, and I want to thank you for helping me draw closer to Him. For taking the time to answer my many questions. The times you spent with me to help guide me in the right direction towards Him. I will not forget, nor let you down. I still remember what you told me about accepting things as they are and that blessings will follow. I'm still thanking God for every detail of my life. I surrender to him daily. I finally got to go to a Bible study here, and because of your Virtual Chapels, I was able to answer some of the questions that came up. That really felt good. I can honestly say that I am happy, even in here, because of my relationship with God. I don't understand everything yet, but I'm content. God bless and take care.

(from a state prison in Delano, California)

Dear Pastor Gerry: I'm a lifer here . . . and one of the other men here passed on one of your books to me. . . The teachings are awesome! I've shared your teachings with others here. Your book has helped me, and my roommates understand Bible doctrine. . . . Thank you for giving us the "meat and potatoes." The book and studies are very detailed—great! . . . I do not know of any other authors who put the Word of God in a simplified manner that is easy for all of us to understand. We (my roommates and me) prefer your books and the studies you send us over all the other studies we get. . . . May the Lord bless your ministry—In Jesus' name I pray.

(from Chowchilla Prison, California)

Dear Pastor: I am 24 years old . . . serving 22 years to life for second degree murder with gang enhancements. I write this letter because a fellow inmate has blessed me with your book on science and origins and your Virtual Chapels. I am truly grateful for them and also knowing such worthwhile material exists. I'm writing to ask if I can be added to your mailing list in case either I or this other inmate gets moved. I don't want to lose touch with your sending the Word of God. I thank God for your family and the people helping you.

(from San Quentin Prison, California)

Pastor: I want to thank you, your wife, and whoever else helps you getting these Virtual Chapels out to me. I can tell you that they are enjoyed by many here, and also the book you sent . . . it is somewhere among the other men right now. As these years go by, and you keep sending in God's Word, many of us have turned our lives over to God. I have just become our resident chaplain to the men in this dorm, and we use your weekly studies often. I believe God is leading me to continue in ministry when I get out . . . to connect with young people and tell them a story that only ends with God. I may be here many more years, but as you say . . . God can use us wherever we are planted . . . or end up . . . I believe!

(from Vacaville Prison, California)

Dear Pastor Gerry: I am reading your book *Revelation, End Times, and This Generation* for the second time, and I love it. You have confirmed a lot of my beliefs. We in prison especially look forward to the return of Jesus . . . and how these times we live in seem to point to our generation—the prophecies being fulfilled even now during our lifetimes. Praise God, we can be at peace and enjoy salvation right here . . . right now!

(from Chowchilla Prison, California)

Dear Pastor Gerry: I received your book along with your Virtual Chapel study yesterday, and they are greatly appreciated. I'll pass the book along as soon as I finish it. Believe it or not, there is a line waiting to read it already. This is a difficult time of year in this place and your letters, books, and studies help more than you know.

(from Folsom Prison, California)

Well chaplain, they got me in the lowest level here . . . down deep in the dark . . . in more ways than one. It is really bad here in the lowest level, and Satan is very much active here. But I must thank you for your Virtual Chapels and the book you sent. Each week when the Virtual Chapels come, there are about 20 down here who can't wait to get their turn to read them in. When possible, we pass them around so that [they] won't get destroyed by those who oppose Christ. Your messages have established a secret society down here . . . we're meeting in the catacombs you might say. It is hard to get deep studies like yours that have real meat in them for us to study and learn. We keep all of your chapels in a pile in a safe cell and go back to them from time to time. Please keep them coming. God bless your ministry.

(from San Quentin Prison, California)

Dear Pastor: I'm sending this to let you know how much I love your messages . . . please keep them coming. With reading your studies, and using the Bible alongside, I find my heart is opening a little more each day to God. I've found that in order to be open for God to come into my life I have to find a way to open my heart to love. I have found that I was going through life thinking I was open to love, when in reality I was just faking it. I am beginning to see light at the end of the tunnel. Don't get me wrong—I'm not there yet, but I'm striving for it. I really hope God will use me and my testimony to help others . . . peace be with you.

(from a state prison in Texas)

Pastor Gerry: You knew I was Jewish when you sent me your Virtual Chapel on Hanukkah . . . yes? One of the inmates here said he got it too. He is a Christian, so I guess you just sent it out. It was very informative for us all here. Anyway, you have been so important to my last five years here . . . May God bless your ministry to us out here.

(Note that the Hanukkah message he was referring to was also broadcast on over 100 Christian radio stations and I also was asked to present it to a Messianic Jewish community on their Sabbath at Hanukkah).

(from a state prison in New Hampshire)

Dear Pastor Gerry: Can't thank you enough for all you have done for me in my life. . . . Been here three days and brought my first person to Christ. I had him speak the words of accepting Jesus into his life as Lord and Savior out loud. Without you and Pastor David I would not be at this place in life. Praise God! I'm spreading the Virtual Chapels and other books and materials you send each week around here. . . . They are greatly appreciated . . . and I have a couple of guys to add to your weekly mailing list. . . . Too bad the postage rates are going up— May God provide. Thanks again, your brother in Christ

(from a newly ordained pastor on the mission field—in prison!)

Hi there, Gerry: It's me . . . I first came in just before 9/11, so it has been many years now I've been away. Hope and pray all is okay and going well. I've been back here in prison for about two months now and am settling in again. As you know, I won't live long enough to serve out my sentence, but I do find it very encouraging to be about ministry, and you are a big part of that, equipping me in understanding God and His plan for us all—His forgiveness, and now opportunities to share with others before I die. Anyway, just wanted to connect with you again. . . . Prayer coming your way . . . in the love of our Lord Jesus.

(from Avenal State Prison, California)

Hello Pastor Gerry: Well, I'm here and very glad you were able to give me some idea of what to expect, and how to rely upon God and not on myself here—How true!!! Another inmate here had a National Graphic, and it reminded me of you always bringing in good stuff to read and get us through each and every day. That is especially true now here— isolated and alone 23 hours a day until I get sent to a permanent place. I appreciate that you took time to meet with my two sons a couple of years ago, and that they are able to reach out to you. They are good boys and hopefully will not go the way of this world. Thank you and God bless.

(from San Quentin Prison, California)

Greetings, Pastor Gerry: I have been getting your Virtual Chapels for several months now, but I don't recall ever meeting you. I was in Quentin for several months, and many times we would pray for a Chaplain Gerry, and then sometimes we would do a study that the other inmates said that a Chaplain Gerry had given them. I assumed that Chaplain Gerry was our local San Quentin chaplain . . . I never saw a chaplain there, but I knew there were some. I didn't realize that all along the San Quentin chaplain was you (virtually, that is). I found out that one of the guys at Quentin had sent you my mailing info. Thank you so much for connecting with me here at Folsom. . . . Again, there are Chaplain's here, but in four months, I have yet to see one. I have several questions concerning the Holy Spirit enclosed here, and hope to hear from you. In God's love.

(from Folsom Prison, California)

Pastor Gerry: I've been baptized, and just finished reading the whole Bible—all of it! My first language is Spanish, so I hope this letter is readable. I met another inmate here who shared with me one of your books, as well as a couple of your Virtual Chapels. I am very interested in receiving your messages and studies. Yours truly.

(from Soledad State Prison, California)

Dear Gerry: First, let me thank you for your writings and books over the last five years. They've helped me have a different insight on things in my life. Also, the others here can't thank you enough for being here for us all these years, as most of us just get lost in the system, moving from prison to prison. I'll be coming home this summer and will be homeless with no clothes, etc., but I have learned to ask God for my needs and to surrender everything to Him. But perhaps you could help me find a transition program or home to help me get on the right foot. Thanks again and peace.

(from Delano State Prison, California)

Pastor Gerry: Up until last week, I was able to read your weekly messages and your books because another inmate here got them and shared them with all of us. But he got sent to a Texas prison, and now we don't get your messages. I have come to know the Lord in the past year and would greatly like to further my walk. If possible, could you add me to your weekly mailing list. There are several of us here who will share them together if at least one of us can get them.

(from Los Angeles State Prison, California)

Dear Pastor Gerry: I found a book here left behind by someone who got out, and I would really like to get more information from your ministry. We have a Bible study group here that uses your weekly messages and books, but the person getting them just got released. My life is changing, and I would like to receive more light, meaning that I would like to start getting your messages so that we here can grow in the faith in Jesus Christ. May God bless your ministry.

(from San Quentin Prison, California)

Hello Pastor Gerry: Can't thank you enough for sending me your messages . . . and the book is terrific. Would you be able to send my husband anything? I'll include the prison address where he is, just in case you can. I cannot help him, but I know God can. I do not want to contact him at this point, but I do love him and pray that he will surrender to Jesus. I am in the process of breaking my co-dependency upon him and trusting in Jesus totally instead. Thanks again for your messages. . . . We share them together all the time here . . . God bless you.

(from Chowchilla Women's Prison, California)

Dear Target Truth Ministries: Another inmate here handed me one of your messages when we were talking about creation. I would very much like to be added to your ministry list. I was OK until I started to do weed. That led to selling drugs. Now that I am here in prison and seeing how God does really love us . . . not like the street. . . . I really want to change my life. My mother is in ministry helping with the food bank down south. I'm her only child, and I have failed her. But I can see from your messages that the answer lies with knowing God. I hope I can get added to your mailings, and many of us here will be blessed each week. God bless.

(from Wasco Prison, California)

Pastor Gerry: I have been reading your Virtual Chapels that others have received for years now. I used to just look at the comics, but then realized that many of them have to do with the messages you write. I began studying the Bible passages you wrote about and looking them up, and I can't thank you enough because they took me to places I never knew existed. I wonder if you can add me to your mailing list, so I don't miss any messages you send out. Thanks for all you do.

(from San Quentin Prison, California)

Pastor Gerry: I've been transferred to this place and had to spend a couple of months in lockdown because my paperwork didn't catch up. Now I'm sending you my new address in hopes I can continue to get your messages. Your messages about God's love for even us in prison, and the reconciliation we can have in Jesus have gotten me through these past couple of months in lock down— just knowing I would be able to get out of this situation and begin getting back into God's Word again. I actually prayed that I might come to this prison because I felt that God could use me here. I've become aware that God can use us for His purpose even in these prisons. I really need your studies to help us here as we begin group studies. Please thank all those who work with you and help you in this ministry to us in prison . . . Yours in Christ!

(from High Desert Prison, California)

Chaplain Gerry: Thanks for all these years of faithfulness. I pray God continues to richly bless you in your ministry. I'll close by asking you to remove me from your book list. I still would like your weekly messages, but I am only allowed so many books. You have been great about sending me a new Christian book every year. I value how you spend your resources, and I want you to mail books to others so they can grow in the faith like me. I'm now very involved in ministry inside these walls and want others to be blessed like I have [been]. God bless you and those who help you and I thank you for all you do.

(from Chowchilla Prison, California)

Pastor Gerry: After all these years that you have stayed in touch with me, well, my life is truly changed. . . . I'm not sure how people will react to someone who has been in prison all these years, but I do know from your studies and messages that real Christians

THE LETTERS

recognize that we were once walking in the world's ways and now are transformed. . . . Thanks again, and please pray for me getting back into society after all these years away.

(from Chino Prison, California)

Dear Pastor Burney: At Christmastime, some of the other cellies here were passing around your Christmas messages, and I found them very interesting . . . made me rethink my thoughts about the Bible and God. Could you add me to your list of people getting your studies? One of the men here also had a book of yours, and I saw on the back cover that you have a book on science and origins. I'm very interested in science, and I must admit that my high school science taught me all about evolution and how the Bible could never be true. But, since I've been reading your messages, I believe you have answered many of my questions. I believe your book could really help a lot of us here who learned only part of the evidence in school. Hope your new year is good to you and your family.

85

(from Tehachapi State Prison, California)

Brothers and Sisters at Target Truth Ministries.com: Praise God for all you do for us here in Texas. We do enjoy your messages very much and know that you send out books once a year. Several of the men here are on your mailing list, which is a good thing as they keep moving us around the state. If possible, we would like the Book of Chronologies and Time Charts. We are studying the end times and the description of your book says that part of it is an outline of how the end times might happen. Your messages are very valuable to our study of the Bible here. Thanks in advance.

(from Huntsville State Prison, Texas)

Pastor: I am a 30-year-old Hispanic serving 37 to life. I am struggling with my faith, and I found one of your messages lying around. I am writing to ask for more messages to help me with my great depression. I believe, as you said, that God can use me even in

this suffocating, negative environment—
but I need help. Please give me hope and a
message from the Holy Spirit. I'm hoping
your messages will help me find the words
necessary to overcome the doubts that the
enemy throws at me all the time.

(from Ione State Prison, California)

Dear Pastor Burney: I receive your Virtual
Chapels and have a new address. I want you
to keep sending me these hopefully. Many
of us use these messages every week in our
devotionals. I got the book "Eden to Evil:
The Puzzle of Creation Explained" you sent
me. Wow! We found it filled with insightful
information and a lot of help. Bless all those
who support your ministry to us in these
dark places.

(from Chowchilla State Prison, California)

Mr. Burney: I recently read your science and
origins book that another inmate here had,
and I loved it. The way you broke down the
science and backed up the facts was very

impressive. . . . I have just started my prison term and now have decided to consider this my missionary trip for the Lord. I see my time here as an opportunity to do His work. I passed your book on to others here, and we all noticed that you have other books and also offer weekly chapel messages. Is it possible to get these? We have no money, but perhaps several of us could pool our stamps and mail some stamps to you, if you need. I'm praying for myself to really develop a very personal relationship with Jesus. Please keep all of us in your prayers, and we will keep you in ours!

(from Coalinga State Prison, California)

Pastor: Here in prison on a federal charge and heard about your book on science and origins, and I have struggled with evolution and God forever. I am indigent and get eight stamps each month, and I'm including all eight in the hopes that you can send me a copy and add me to your mailing list for what you call Virtual Chapels because there is currently no Bible studies being done here from outside. I'll send more stamps next month, too. Respectfully.

(from Lafayette Prison, Mississippi)

(Note we used the stamps he sent after this communication with him but informed him it was not necessary to send more).

Dear Pastor Gerry: Ever since my brother committed suicide at age 20, I've been hooked on meth. Now I'm 55 and back in here and what do I get me second day here? One of your messages from another inmate here. Your messages and books over the years have caused me to rethink my life . . . and getting this one on my second day back in is like God telling me to wake up. I just want to thank you for God's messages and the years I did in jail, and for you staying in touch with me over the years. I hope you will continue and add me back onto your mailing list. . . I pray this time will be different . . . It feels that way already as I surrender to God for real! God bless you my brother.

(from San Quentin Prison, California)

Dear Chaplain: We use your messages here every day to answer many questions about faith. I want to thank you for your personal testimony. It has enriched my faith. When I get out, I hope I can still get your messages and share them with others at home. I do not think I can get back together with my husband because he seems to resist God and church. He also is in prison, and I am including his address hoping that you can add him and his cellmates onto your mailing list. I believe the way you write about God will get through to him, as he has shown interest from time to time. I cannot contact him right now—not unless he seeks God. Thank you for your ministry, and send our thanks to all those who support this ministry, too—OK?

(from a women's prison)

Pastor Gerry: Thanks for the information on a transition program for when I get out. . . . I struggle between my Apache background and my family who are mostly Christian. . . . Your messages over the years have helped me and others here understand our Lord and Savior. I want to be a good father for my children when I return . . . Written with respect.

(from a state prison in California)

Chaplain Gerry: Guess what? Oh boy, do I have news for you! I want to thank you for working with me. . . . Thanks for helping me get into a Christian recovery home. Been here about six months now. Yes, I'm a new product of God's grace. Today, I'm reaching out to you to invite you to my baptism. . . . I'm really excited and you are a big part of my journey. I am now a God-fearing woman with so much confidence, knowing I have a purpose in life with my love of God. Hope to see you.

(from Victory Outreach Women's Recovery Home, New Mexico)

Pastor Gerry: Thank you so much for sending me more of your Virtual Chapels. Please pray for the negative, combative people that surround me. Please pray for my family that has disowned me—that they soften their hearts. Please pray for my husband who has given into drugs because of all the death he experienced while serving in Iraq. I believe God will turn his life around as God is changing my life, and I pray for that.

(from a woman's state prison)

Dear Gerry: Thanks for the book *God's Plan/ Satan's Plan* you sent. We all here at Corcoran Prison enjoy the monthly messages and especially the cartoons you put in. God's blessing upon you. . . . In Jesus' name.

(from Corcoran Prison, California)

Gerry: My best wishes to you and your wife. How is everyone at the local jail doin'? Today is Thanksgiving here in prison, and I just wanted you to know that I will forever be thankful to have you in my life. You helped me a lot when I was having a tough time. God led you to me and made a true difference in my life. Just thought I'd spend time with someone I love and appreciate. God bless, and always in my prayers.

(from a state prison)

Chaplain Gerry: It means a lot to this Christian to receive a letter which contains guidance to further my walk with our Lord and Savior. I have been reading the two studies that you sent me. There is so much written, and the explanation is well understood. A few of the other brothers here have sent a message of thanks to you also. I am more than willing to help in any way I can, as I hate for today's youth to have to go through all I have done and seen. May God bless you.

(from a former gang member)

Dear Mr. Burney: I have been getting your weekly messages for five months now. I appreciate your hard work and willingness to reach out to those in need with the Word. I'm sure this jail will miss you a lot and all your efforts to ensure the inmates have books, magazines, and a weekly message. I am glad to see you are entering into a new chapter in your life, and I hope that wherever the Lord takes you, you will be filled with happiness and lovingkindness. Please add me to your list so I don't miss out on anything. God bless.

(Mendocino County Jail, Ukiah)

RACING DAYS

Right about the same time that Monica and I became a couple, I was transitioning from competitive running to road racing. In the beginning, I was not very competitive at all, as cycling uses a different set of leg muscles than running, and there is a whole different kind of strategy involved in bike racing. Every time I got pulled out of a race (due to having been lapped by the top racers) or was one of the very last to finish, I told our kids that this was part of my job as a parent—to teach them humility. Believe me, I gave them many examples to observe my being a gracious loser in those early days of bike racing.

Race ready: Gerry and fellow teammate, Will Carson, raced in the World Corporate Games in the Bay Area in 1989. The following year, Gerry and teammate Leonard Ke (the "flyin' Hawaiian") competed in the Games in Leonard's home state of Hawaii.

Over time, however, I got up to speed with cycling. Even with all that my body had been through in that severe accident at age twenty-five, I was still able to push myself to extreme limits and persevere in my goals. We traveled to bike races all over Northern California, but we also went to the Central Valley and Southern California. A few times we also traveled out of state for stage races, national championships and the World Corporate Games. We also followed the now defunct Coors Classic race from San Francisco to Boulder, Colorado.

Gerry and Will were not only training partners and bike club teammates, they also both worked at the same phone company building, but in different departments.

Bear Valley, California: One of many memorable races in heavily snow-laden places.

Gentlemen, start your engines! Although Gerry competed in a number of time trials, criteriums, and circuit races over the years, his niche was to race in the long, grueling road races. To his way of thinking, the steeper and longer the climb, the better.

Gerry's friend, Roger Moore, custom made a bike rack to accommodate Gerry' racing bikes. Many passersby looked in amazement at how such a small, compact vehicle could haul such cargo.

I also realized a special goal of mine—to compete in the Master's World Cycling Championships near Innsbruck, Austria. As I mentioned previously, our oldest daughter, Vanessa, was getting married in Lucca, Italy, in the summer of 2006. I had the special honor of officiating the wedding ceremony. After we left Lucca, our younger daughter, Hillary, joined us, and we traveled to several other countries. Every day when we left to go sightseeing, I'd jokingly comment, "Well, I guess we're off to see another pile of old bricks."

Master's World Championships in St. Johann in Tirol (near Innsbruck, Austria) in 2006.

It was, of course, far more than that. Having previously traveled back east with our daughters while they were in high school, seeing all the iconic historical sights of our nation's humble beginnings, it was truly a stark contrast to see just how much further back European history goes and how well-preserved so many of the historical sites still are.

Over the years, I had many victories in my racing. I also had some bad crashes and suffered some serious injuries. One such year, I was in a phone company school for two weeks in Southern California. On the weekend in between the two weeks, I entered a bike race. I crashed and broke my collarbone. I was able to get myself to the hospital but was actually given the wrong kind of sling to help with recovery. On Monday, I was back at the phone company school and another guy at the training (who was a motorcyclist and had crashed and broken his collarbone before) told me on our break that what I needed was a butterfly sling. So I went to a store that sold healthcare aids and purchased the right kind of sling. It was still a painful process, but the sling helped my collarbone heal more correctly.

Years later, I was on a training ride one afternoon on a steep, mountainous road not far from home. It was a windy day. I liked training on this road because it was a steep enough incline to really challenge me and didn't have a lot of traffic. It was rather dangerous because there were blind curves and not much shoulder. There was a steep cliff on one side and a rocky wall of mountain on the other side of the road. I caught the wind with my wheel in what is called a high speed wobble. This occurred just as a car was approaching from both the front and another from behind me. Choosing the rocky wall to the sheer drop off, I crashed.

The cars stopped to see if I was okay. My bike was damaged, and I was in shock. I waved off the offers of help and said I was just a little banged up but would be fine. When I surveyed the damage on my bike, I decided I better not take a chance going down the hill on a broken wheel. I called Monica and asked her to come pick me up. When she arrived, she asked if she should take me to the hospital. Having gone through the John Wayne school of True Grit, I shunned the idea and said that all I needed was to go home and take a hot shower.

After I got out of the shower, I realized whatever was wrong, I would not easily shake it off. The shower helped me realize how banged up I really was. We went to the hospital and the triage nurse asked what my pain level was. I told her a five. My high tolerance for pain doesn't always serve me well. They ended up taking others in before me, and we ended up waiting an extended amount of time to be seen. When the ER doctor finally did see me, it turned out I had five broken ribs, two broken bones in my shoulder blade, yet another broken collarbone, and a punctured lung. They cleaned and dressed my broken bones as best they could and kept me overnight to monitor the punctured lung. I was released late the next morning. I slept sitting up in a chair for two weeks until it was manageable to sleep horizontally again.

The very next year, I was on a training ride with my friend Al in a neighboring town. He was fifty yards ahead of me at the time of this incident. There was a bend in the road ahead of me that went to the left but had a private road going straight. If I had gone straight (instead of following the bend), it would have taken me onto a private road. A seemingly older gentleman (he was actually only sixty-five, just a few years younger than I was at the time) came along behind me in his car and assumed that I was going to head straight onto the private road, as he was. Very presumptuous! As I followed the curve in the road and he went straight, he hit me, knocking me to the ground. He drove as some older people do when they start losing their edge and make faulty judgments in their driving.

My friend heard the crash and came back to assist me. He called the California Highway Patrol (CHP). The officer who responded was someone we knew from our daughter's youth group years before. He asked me the typical questions to assess my condition. "What is your name?" "Do you know what day it is?" "Do you know your age?" I was clearly in shock and could not answer the questions accurately. The CHP officer called for an ambulance and offered to take my bike back to our home since he knew where we lived. My friend called Monica and told her what had happened. He met her at the hospital to give her more details of the accident and to make sure I was going to be okay. Sure enough, more broken bones and this time, a concussion, and a long healing process.

At age sixty-eight, I received an invitation from the organizers of the Rock 'n Roll Las Vegas Marathon to enter the fiftieth anniversary race to be held in a year and a half. I hadn't run in many years, but being the competitor that I am, I was intrigued by the challenge. I began training and had many setbacks along the way. I really had to pace myself, easing back into the sport.

Fortunately, I had a wide berth of time to prepare. Unlike that first marathon I ran at age twenty, I would be seventy years old at this race.

Gerry, Vanessa, and Hillary after the Great Giant Race at ATT ballpark in San Francisco (2014).

Reflecting back in 1967, I ran in Hush Puppies. There were no special running shoes at that time. There were also no aid stations on the course. There were no rock concerts at different venues along the course. There was no live coverage and paparazzi everywhere. Running was not a big sport back then, so the spectators were few.

In 2016, it was somewhat of a family affair. I knew Vanessa was planning to also run the marathon. Her two friends from Burney, who had never run a 10K before, also planned to enter the race. Unfortunately, Vanessa had bronchitis weeks before and lost valuable training time, so she opted to run the half-marathon instead. What I didn't know was that Hillary flew in from Sicily to surprise me at the airport. I thought we were going to meet only Vanessa and Gracie there. She was going to run the 10K! To have almost our entire family there to cheer us on (Monica; Mike; our daughter-in-law, Katie; our youngest grandchildren, Nate and Gracie—minus our grandson Ryan) was far more than I had hoped for.

Running crew: Amanda, Marisa, Vanessa, Gerry, and Hillary just prior to their races in the Rock 'n' Roll race in Las Vegas, Nevada (November 2016).

Marathon Man: Gerry running in the fiftieth anniversary of the Las Vegas marathon at age seventy. At the finish line, he was swarmed by paparazzi who treated him with star status as they photographed and interviewed him for completing the race with distinction.

They closed down the Strip, and the races began in the late afternoon. The 10K racers started at a different location than the half and full marathoners. The guy who initially was declared the winner in my age category was disqualified because he cut the course short by five miles. A guy from France came in first place. A runner from Belgium finished in second. I finished in third place overall in the 70-74 age (and the first American). I was given special attention after I finished because I was the only marathoner from the inaugural race to come back again fifty years later and finish the race at age seventy. They interviewed me, photographed me, and made a short video of my story.

Although I am quite sure I will never run another marathon, I am glad to have had that experience, especially with my family. The next year, our grandson Nate challenged me to run in the 10K category in the very same Las Vegas Rock 'n'Roll. To this day, I continue to train for 10K races and maintain my conditioning for bike racing (though my racing days are winding down, since there are so few races that have a category for my age group).

In 2017, grandson Nate (a non-runner), challenged his Grandpa Gerry to run the 10K in the Las Vegas Rock 'n' Roll race.

Racing has taught me some valuable life lessons about humility, dedication, patience, endurance, and how fearfully and wonderfully made our human bodies are. As a believer in Jesus Christ, I know that I am made in God's image (see Gen. 1:26) and that my body is the temple of the living God (see 1 Cor. 6:19). I have marveled at how a body so greatly impacted by concussions, a devastating accident, and numerous bike crashes can, at seventy-six years old, still push the limits to the extreme and be as healthy as I am.

Christmas Eve day 2021, I had the opportunity to go back to Memorial Hospital in Santa Rosa and meet with some staff and thank them for the work they did and to testify to what God has done in my life since that fateful day fifty years ago when He spared me for a kingdom purpose. It was a personal blessing to me to encourage them and share my story with them. It had been a couple of very difficult years for these valiant workers through the pandemic we experienced. These unsung heroes always put their lives at risk, make sacrifices (like giving up time with their families on holidays) to care for strangers who they will never see again. I am grateful for them, and I am proud to share that our daughter Vanessa went on to become one of them as she graduated the nursing program at Santa Rosa Junior College and was hired on at Memorial Hospital as an RN. We are so incredibly proud of her, especially with the personal hardships she endured putting herself through school as a single parent and enduring some setbacks with her schooling due to the pandemic.

A NEW SEASON

As I look back, I can clearly see God's hand upon my life all through these many years of highs and lows and everything in between. I am so grateful that He didn't give up on me. I'm thankful that He directed the ER staff not to give up on me. I'm still amazed that He would choose to use me when for the first almost forty years of my life I ignored Him and chased after worldly pleasures. I am humbled that despite my many failings, He saw value in me and gave me assignments I felt unworthy to carry out. Over time, He unfolded a beautiful plan before my eyes that resulted in many lives coming to faith in Jesus and leaving old, destructive paths behind.

Both Monica and I have suffered the loss of losing both of our parents. I was blessed to have spent time with my dad as he was dying of cancer and especially blessed to lead him to the Lord two days before his passing. Since then, Monica and I have had many discussions about life and death issues. Especially as we are in a new season in our lives, one that requires us to address the fact that we are getting older, and we know whether the Lord returns in our lifetime or not, we are in our own end time on this earth. The clock is ticking, and it is our heart's desire to make every moment count for the cause of Christ. We were put here for a purpose—to glorify our risen Lord and King! We see the events of human history coming to a climax. This earth, too, shall pass. In the meantime, there are so many still going through life without hope, without the Savior. Even though we can't save anybody, God has sent us to be His messengers, His hands and feet to deliver His message of love, hope, and truth.

Steve, Gerald Sr., and Gerry in Green Valley, Arizona. Gerry's parents lived there for a while before moving back to Santa Rosa. Gerry had the privilege of leading his dad to the Lord just a few days before his dad passed.

God tells us in Revelation 20:8, that an astounding number of people will perish and spend all eternity separated from their Creator. They will be "like the sand on the seashore." This very fact both saddens me and frightens me for them. Yet we are also told, "The harvest is plentiful, but the workers are few" (Matt. 9:37). This verse motivates me and encourages me to keep looking for opportunities to boldly share my faith.

In 2022, I officially stepped down from being chaplain for sixteen years. But the word *retirement* is not in my vocabulary! I will continue to send Virtual Chapels to inmates at our local jail who request them, take these messages to Juvenile Hall every Sunday morning, and mail them also to prisoners at facilities all across the country along with the books I have written. I will continue to bring the devotional at the Center for Hope and encourage these downtrodden souls, whose lives have been decimated by addictions and other dysfunctions.

Of all places to serve, Mendocino County is a notable mecca for drugs in the entire nation. It is only second to neighboring Lake County in drug overdoses in California. We've had members of the Russian mafia in our jail. We've just learned of a pastor's son who died at eighteen from a Fentanyl overdose. We're seeing more and more evidence of gang activity ramping up with graffiti and crime spiking. The trafficking problem continues to increase as well. Despite all this, it is not fear that motivates me—it's hope. I know what it is to have hope and what it is like to live without it. As long as I draw breath, I will testify to God's life-giving message to anyone who will listen.

I would have loved to have continued on at the jail for years to come. Unfortunately, my hearing problem continued to get worse. Part of my hearing loss can be attributed to my time in Vietnam and part of it was due to the ear infection I had that was misdiagnosed. Years ago, a local ear, nose, and throat doctor sent me to the hospital at Stanford. Originally, they thought I had Meniere's disease, as my inner ear was causing me to feel dizzy and nauseous more and more. It was becoming debilitating to where I'd have to stay in bed for a day or two.

While at Stanford, they did a battery of tests and then informed me that it was not Meniere's and that they could help me. At the time, I only had about eight percent hearing left in my left ear. They said they couldn't improve my hearing in that ear, because the damage was already done. They could stop the problem I was having from wreaking havoc with my equilibrium, though. They put a giant shot in my ear, while I was fully awake—Ouch! I have a very high tolerance for pain, but it was extremely painful. Since I had so little hearing left in that ear, they said by killing what hearing was left, my brain's signals would not be confused by my faulty hearing on the left side any longer.

If the shot didn't take the first time, they could try two more times, with a month break in between shots. After the first shot, I had some episodes where I would suddenly drop to the ground with no warning. One of the times, I caught the sharp corner of a metal table and still have a large scar on my back as a result. The next month, we went back to Stanford for the second shot. It worked! I am now completely deaf in my left ear, but I no longer have problems with vertigo-like symptoms.

In 2020, my right ear started experiencing major hearing loss as well. I went to the Santa Rosa VA, and the audiologist determined that I was a good candidate for a cochlear implant. I was sent to the San Francisco VA and had the surgery at the beginning of December. After the incision had time to heal, the device was activated on our wedding anniversary on December 31, 2020. It has helped tremendously, but hearing is still a challenge in very noisy environments, such as the jail.

I am thankful for the technology that improved my hearing so that I can still communicate reasonably well. I am also grateful for the good care I have received through the VA. I most likely will need a cochlear in my right ear at some point down the road. I also have been diagnosed with memory loss from all of the trauma my brain has endured over the years. No matter how bad things get, I still feel blessed to have the health I have at seventy-six years old. It can always be worse. I'm still out there training for running and bike races. I'm still writing Virtual Chapels and updating my books. I have a wonderful family and have a very fulfilling life.

I am really enjoying this new season of life, as every season offers its own unique gifts and surprises. Like Paul, I've come to a place in my life where I can truthfully say, "I have learned to be content whatever the circumstances. I know what it is to be in need, and I know what it is to have plenty. I have learned the secret of being content in any and every situation" (Phil. 4:11-12).

The secret to living not only a content life but an abundant life is not the things of this earth. Even though I wish I had come into a relationship with Jesus at a much earlier age, I'm glad I finally did meet Him and have committed my life to Him. It has made all the difference in discovering my true purpose in this world—the very reason I was created—to glorify Him with all my heart, soul, mind, and strength (see Mk. 12:30). And although I can take no credit for all the lives I've seen changed (as, again, I'm only a mailman—a vessel to carry the truth of God's Word), being an ambassador for Christ has been such a high privilege and brings me such joy every time I see a life reborn and set free from the bondage of sin.

If you are a believer in the Lord Jesus Christ, I pray that this book has been an encouragement to you. If you have not received the free gift of salvation yet, I hope and pray that my story will cause you to ask the only questions that really matter in this life: Why am I here? What is this life about? Does my life make a difference to others? Is there a God? What happens to me after my life is over? In 1 Chronicles 28:9, God makes it very clear: "If you seek him, he will be found by you; but if you forsake him, he will reject you forever." Giving up control of your life may be the hardest thing you will ever do, but it will also be the best thing you will ever do, leaving no regrets. Surrender your life to God and be amazed what He will do in and through you. You have nothing to lose and everything to gain. May your life become the glorious adventure that God intended for you, and I hope to meet you in heaven one day!

Gerry was the honored officiant at the wedding of son, Mike, and daughter-in-law, Katie.

A joyous celebration at the beautiful Bellagio hotel in Las Vegas, Nevada, for the joining together of Mike and Katie. Little did Gerry know many years before while stationed in Las Vegas, that there would later be so many significant events to bring him back to this city.

It takes "u" to make an "us." Gerry had this message monogrammed on a pillowcase as a sweet reminder to Monica that they are "one flesh" (see Genesis 2:24).

Gerry, Monica, Katie, and Mike at San Diego Safari Park.

Sharing some special time with Mike and grandsons, Ryan and Nate at BeBop's—a popular hamburger spot.

117

December 2016. The family came together for a renewal of vows ceremony to celebrate 30 years of a blessed marriage.

The love story continues . . .

ABOUT THE AUTHOR

Monica Burney is a pastor's wife who has served as a ministry leader in several areas of church life: Women's ministry director, Children's Ministry director, Church Secretary, and Bible memory resource consultant. She is an award-winning author and poet whose works have spanned several genres: author, poet, songwriter, columnist, and free-lance journalist. She resides in Northern California. She and her husband, Gerry, have three children and three grandchildren.